"The Little Angel"

THOMAS KRUGER
(THE POET)

ISBN 978-1-0980-4243-1 (paperback)
ISBN 978-1-0980-4244-8 (digital)

Copyright © 2020 by Thomas Kruger (The Poet)

All rights reserved. No part of this publication may be reproduced, distributed, or transmitted in any form or by any means, including photocopying, recording, or other electronic or mechanical methods without the prior written permission of the publisher. For permission requests, solicit the publisher via the address below.

Christian Faith Publishing, Inc.
832 Park Avenue
Meadville, PA 16335
www.christianfaithpublishing.com

Printed in the United States of America

United Together Forever

A smile melts the coldest heart
A friend is one that will always be there,
With kind words, a hand shake, or a hug
They will reach out and let you know that they care

Whether male or female
We, each and every one, need a friend,
And that friend can be a man or a woman
That with comfort will ease those trials that the world has placed within

Many friends have I had in my day
But I've only had four of best of friends in my life,
Three of which are now gone
And the other one has health problems, both he and his wife

I lost my soul mate on June twenty-fifth two thousand eighteen
She was my wife and love of my life for sixty-two years,
It hurts deep within my heart and I miss her so very much
That my soul within is drowning with tears

I know that we will reunite again one day
Up there in the promised land,
And she will be like the sister that I've never had
As I give her a hug and walk beside her hand in hand

Filled with *Jesus's* love
We will sing together her favorite old familiar song,
As we walk in the garden
And the angels chime in with us and sing along

My heart yearns for the coming of that day
When we walk in that beautiful garden of Eden,
As we as sister and brother with each other and with Jesus
Unite together forever with him

P.T.L. #1646 2-8-2019

O Yes, Lord

Jesus said:
Tom, will you walk the hallelujah trail of life with me?
And I said, "Yes, *Lord*, O yes, Lord
I will follow you and share your love with others from sea to shining sea

Till my days on earth are over and done
I will honor you with these poems that you have given to me,
And I pray for them to draw others to you
To receive your gift of life that sets souls forever free

Oh what wonders await us
And every repentant soul,
And to all who reach out to grasp hold of *Christ's* love and gift of grace
As they give their all to reach others wherever they go

Peace like a river will flood over your soul
With a mighty gushing powerful flow,
And *God's* blessings will be upon you all your days
Wherever you are and wherever you go

Become a vessel of honor as you serve the *Lord*
Giving all glory and praise to the one who took upon himself your sin,
Giving life a greater purpose for living by reaching out with love
    for others
As you take that closer walk with him

He gives us gifts in which to serve him all our days
Gifts not given for one's self glory,
Gifts to share with others from the holy book
Of the words of life's beginning and end of mother earth's story

We read of his love for us
That took him to that cruel cross,
And of all those who follow him on the road less traveled
As they reach out with him and through him to reach the lost

P.T.L #1647 2-10-2019 *Sunday*

The Gifts

Oh for the gifts that *God* has given
O hallelujah, O hallelue,
O for the gifts that God has given
Given to me and to you

Gifts to fill and to overflow our soul
Wonderful gifts given to draw others in,
Gifts to share the joy of knowing *Jesus*
Gifts given with a beginning without end

Sharing *God's* love through the sharing of these gifts
Gifts that were purchased for us on the cross,
That with his gifts that he has given to us we may reach out to others
Praying that none be ever lost

Praise the *Lord*, O hallelujah
Praise the *Lord*, O hallelue,
God's gifts to the hearts of the redeemed
God's gifts to the hearts and souls of me and you

Some can dance
Some can preach the word.
Some can play an instrument
Some can sing as beautifully as a bird

Oh what a wonderful world that we live in
Since *Jesus* came into our hearts,
As we use those gifts that he has given
Cherishing his solemn promise to never from us ever depart

Music of the soul
Pouring out in unending praises to *Jesus*,
As we give our all of everything
To the one who gave his all for us

P.T.L #1648 2-17-2019 *Sunday*

Every Dawning of Every Day

The word of *God* is quick and powerful
And sharper than any two-edged sword,
All the demons of darkness around us
Cannot stand before the power of our risen *Lord*

No matter where we are
No matter where we go, we need not fear,
For *Jesus* walks beside us and lives inside us
Till that day of being forever with him draws near

He is with us in the good times
And he is with us in the dark times,
He will never leave nor forsake us
O what inspiration he has given to us in these written verses of rhyming lines

He is yours and he is mine
And so shall he forever be,
For with his blood that he shed upon the cross
He still reaches out to set souls free

No matter how bad the circumstances are in life
Take it all to *Jesus* and never give up,
No matter how hard the devil tries to drag us down
Never of converted hearts can he corrupt

We will follow *Jesus* wherever he leads
Wherever he bids us to go,
We are here to share his pure sweet, sweet love with others
And of all of him within our soul we have come to cherish and to know

Every awakening of every dawning of every *God*-given day
And with a prayer overflowing within,
Let us serve the *Lord God* of glory
As he adds his blessings to our praises that we lift up every day with love to him

P.T.L. #1649 3-2-2019

Amen.

Life in Jesus

It's not what's inside that counts
It's what's inside that comes out,
The sharing of *Jesus* with others
Is what life in *Jesus* is all about!

Something this beautiful
Cannot be hidden within,
We've got to reach out
To draw others in

We are vessels of the good news
Of *Jesus* and his gift of saving grace,
Asking him to come into your heart
Gives you a whole new beautiful life to face

We are each given gifts
In which to serve him and draw others in,
And if we do our part
Jesus will do his, my friend

Jesus is not idle
And neither shall we be,
We need to reach out and touch the searching souls
Who *Jesus* draws to him through you and me

Let none be lost
Because we fail his mission,
When *Christ* guides souls to cross our path
Our opportunity has been heavenly given

Yes! It's not what's inside that counts
It's what's inside that comes out,
Sharing *God's* love and compassion with others
Is what life in *Jesus* is all about!

P.T.L. #1650 3-3-2019

The End Is Just the Beginning

When life on earth comes to an end
Make sure you are headed in the right direction,
By bowing down at the altar of grace
To receive forever *God's* eternal love and affection

What is life?
It is but a mist and then it's gone,
It's what we do with it
That guides us to where we are forever going

If we live it right
Washed clean in the blood of *Jesus Christ*,
We will live forever
In the glory of heaven's brilliant golden light

Death
Is only a closing and opening of the eyes,
It's when those eyes open again, as quick as when they closed
That your destination forever materializes

If in the book of life
Your name is written down,
You will be robed in glistening white
And wearing a golden crown

You will sing of the victory
That in *Christ* you have won,
As the angels sing along
In the light brighter than the noon day sun

Gold and ivory everywhere
Beautiful music floating in the air,
Reuniting with Christian friends who have gone on before
To be again wrapped into the arms of their gentle care

I yearn to see *Alice* again
I know that in heaven we will not be husband and wife,
But I will love her like a sister that I never had
And that love will be forever for all our unending eternal life

P.T.L. #1651 3-3-2019

No Greater Joy

The same question that *Jesus* asked *Peter*
Is the same question to us that needs our answer to him,
His question was: do you love me, feed my sheep
Then he repeated it again and again

Are we sharing *God's* love with others?
Are we doing all that we can?
If you know *Jesus* as *Lord* and *Savior*
Reach out and draw others toward his promised land

Share that love
That love that *Jesus* has so freely given,
And it is sure to come back to you many fold
The rest of your life in him that you are now living

Jesus is waiting patiently to bless souls
To bless all who would come and follow him,
He gave his mortal life for all
That we may, through him, receive life without end

With a love far beyond our expectations and imaginations
Jesus gave his all for us,
Then that third day he rose to life again
With a promise of a gift, oh so precious

A gift to all who reach out with open hearts
His promise that in no wise will he cast them out,
His promise to all those who come to him
Those who have no shadows in their hearts of doubt

He will write their names in the book of life
As we, with the angels, give the victory cry,
No greater joy shall we ever know
Than of that day we rise to *Jesus* in those angel-filled beautiful skies

P.T.L. #1652 3-4-2019

Holy Matrimony

God has placed us into time
For a temporal short season,
This world is *God's* proving ground for us
To see if we choose the devil's dark side or live our lives for him

The devil is a very jealous and powerful fallen angel
Who drew a third of the angels down to earth to dwell with him,
He is the great tempter of flesh and soul
When he knocks on your heart's door, do not open up and let him in

He and all who follow him
Will, one day, succumb to the lake of eternal fire,
I pray for all souls who walk this earth
That they would set their eternal goals much higher

Jesus's promises
Are true and are eternal,
Don't walk this earth on the low road
That leads to the devil's fiery infernal

Follow the high and narrow road
With other Christian soldiers hand in hand,
Never faltering and never wavering
All the way to the promised land

When the devil tries to lure you in
Remind him of the one who lives inside,
And that he and his followers have no power to convert your soul
Since you, with sacred vows, were joined together with *Jesus* like a groom and bride

P.T.L. #1653 3-5-2019

Like None Other Shall Ever Be

There is a day coming
Like none other shall ever be,
That day that the angels fill the heavens
And *Jesus* in all his glory we shall see

Hallelujah, hallelujah
What a day of rejoicing that will be,
When with all our loved ones who have gone on before
We reunite together again in *God's* promised land of the redeemed and free

Yes! I said it before and I will say it again, it will be a day like no other shall ever be
With voices lifting up to *God* in praise,
We will rise to our *holy Lord God* of glory
Our blessed creator and *Lord* of endless days

Music will fill the air
As the sound of rejoicing echoes on and on everywhere,
All throughout the heavens the music will be overflowing with praises
And rejoicings to the one who took all our sins to bear

O hallelujah, O hallelujah
Rejoicing voices praising *God* who is always faithful and true,
Never ending praises
Praises rising up into the heavens like the refreshing mist of the morning dew

Heaven
O what a beautiful sight for all that rise to see,
Of all of *God's* blessings that lay before them
From emerald glassy seas to ivory palaces all created for you and me

Golden streets glissading with a glow more glorious than the colored arch of a rainbow
With ivory palaces lined up on each side,
There is no greater treasure that we shall ever know
Than our home in glory where in the presence of *Jesus* we are blessed to forever abide

P.T.L. #1654 3-7-2-19

Nail-pierced Hands

We need *Jesus*
Nothing less and nothing more,
He is the greatest treasure that we could ever have
Nothing less and nothing more

If we walk the narrow line
Doing what *Jesus* would have us to do,
His blessings will continue to flow
And fill that new heart he has placed within you

O what endless joy he gives to us
As we reach out to others through him,
As he convicts souls through us
As he draws the wondering souls in

When we reached out to him we were born again
For heavenly purposes to perform,
As we reach out to those around us
That they may be miraculously reborn

O the joy of knowing *Jesus*
This is too precious to hold within,
Through him we have a mission to perform
Given to us that day that we were born again

He blesses others through us
Through us who are but ashes and dust,
Born again to reach out to others
As we reach out to put their souls in those hands we trust

Pierced hands
Hands that were nailed to the cross,
Only to come back to life that third day
To reach out with the gift of life to the lost

P.T.L. #1655 3-8-2019 *Friday*

The Icing on the Cake

My *Jesus*, O to hear his name not spoken in vain
O how dear he is to my heart,
My *Jesus*, for now and forever, my *Jesus*
Nothing can ever separate us apart

I feel so unworthy to receive such love
But I will cherish it as long as I live,
He gave his all for me
To him my all I give

Poems of praise
All overflowing from a converted heart,
Words, oh so precious words
With the power of the pen I will continue to do my part

With rhyming verse
I pray to touch the world around me,
The Bible's words are stronger than the weapons of destruction
The words in the Bible have the power to convert souls to be set free

The only way I know to get the message out
Is with the love of *Jesus* written on the Bible's sacred pages,
From Genesis to Revelation
The word of *God* has converted souls all down through the ages

The tongue is a mighty weapon
As is also the pen,
You can preach the word or teach the word
But it is *Jesus* who blesses our efforts to draw others in

He is the icing on the cake
He adds his blessings to all we undertake to do,
Just keep on doing what he has blessed you to do
And remember that he will always be there for you

P.T.L. #1656 3-8-2019

Spinning in the Wind

Like a tornado spinning wildly in the wind
Jesus is coming to wrap his arms around us,
As we reach out and place our arms around him

He is coming to take us to our forever home
To unite us with our loved ones once again,
With never ending rejoicing sounding everywhere
Coming from *Jesus* and all our friends and kin

Where joy shall never cease
As we bask in the glory of *Christ's* presence,
Surrounded by holy angels and of those of long ago passing
With no thoughts lingering on, of our lives that are now pastiness

No more time clocks
No such thing as tomorrows,
As spiritual bodies shine on in the glory of *Christ's* presence
To experience no more darkness, pain, nor sorrows

While we were here on earth
We've done our Christian duty with love,
We did it with faithfulness to our maker
As we shared with others *God's* promise of our heavenly home above

O for that never ending joy in that place of no more daylight saving time
In our finite minds this is hard to comprehend,
But having received the fullness of *Jesus's* love
We have been cleansed in the blood, and miraculously born again

I have long waited for those final bells for me to toll
In anxious joy and anticipation,
Praying for all those that I will leave behind
And for the United States of America to continue to be a Christian nation

P.T.L. #1657 3-9-2019

In the Light of Higher Ground

You have touched my heart and soul, *Lord*
You have placed within me a greater purpose in life,
You have given me a divine goal for living
Through these verses you inspire me to write

There is no other fount I know
That can quench the thirst of a searching soul,
Than when they drink from the cup of life
And the blessings within and without begin to flow

Eternal life
Is only to be found in the blood of the cross,
Jesus, the sacrificial lamb
Is the only cure that can save the lost

We who are saved
Were saved to serve the living *Christ*,
He has given us a mission
To serve him all the rest of our life

We are not to waste the opportunities that he places before us
Of the searching souls he guides to cross our paths,
We are to use of that which he has given
To the full and with all else of that which we have

I once was lost
But now am found,
I once walked in the valley of the shadow
But now I walk in the light of higher ground

He opened my eyes
That I may see,
And opened my heart
And set me free

P.T.L. #1658 3-14-2019 *Thursday*

The Awakening of Spring

The hills and valleys both high and low
Woods and fields bursting forth with colors all aglow,
The land like quilts of coverings blanketing the earth
As rainbow-colored flowers spread out everywhere we go

Bursting forth amongst the pussy willows with a colorful display
Along with the delicious morel mushrooms,
The leaves return to restore and clothe the naked trees
As the big bullfrogs sound off with their base drum loony tunes

Springtime brings life back to earth again
As the ice melts from off every pond and lake,
The bluegills are fanning out oval pockets
As the little peepers of the ponds add their concerto
Of springtime's music, luring the earth again to awake

It's time to get the fly rod out again
And that little solo canoe,
And the spinning rod too
To cast out and catch a bass or two

It is time to hike those old familiar trails again
As everything continues to burst forth in life all around you,
The pussy willows are beginning to bloom
As also the redbuds and the dogwoods begin to take form with life again

Beauty unsurpassed
As life restores its self again upon the earth,
Revealing its self before our awestruck eyes
As we watch winter give way to springtime's yearly birth

It is a time of rejoicing of spring's arrival
It is time to get out and enjoy life again,
A time to camp, a time to fish, and time to get outside
To play, to travel, or just to get out to take a swim

P.T.L. #1659 3-22-2019

As True as the Sky Is Blue

If you have never come to an altar of grace
Make this day a day of new beginning
As you look forward to that home of a better place

It is time to give life a new start,
Reach out to *Jesus*
And receive his gift of a new heart

Life will become worth living
And death will not look to be so sad and drear,
For on the other side of that dark valley of death
Is never a drop of a tear

A place where you will be welcomed home
By the holy *God* of three yet one,
Father, *Son*, and *Holy Ghost*
And all the holy angels singing glory in the highest for the victory
 that you have won

Let the light shine in as you live your life for *Christ*
And let it shine out to draw others in,
Rejoicing for *God's* gift to you of grace
And a home of that awesome place of no end

Heaven, the Bible only gives us a glimpse of what's over there
A beautiful place unsurpassed by no other,
Where we will unite again with those who have gone on before
Of relatives, friends, acquaintances, and every Christian sister and brother

In God's home is where we shall forever abide
It is all so wonderful and so hard to fully comprehend,
But this is as true as the sky is blue
Believe it and reach out and receive it
It is where all our hopes and dreams come true

P.T.L. #1660 3-27-2019 *Wednesday*

A Tug on the Pants' Leg and upon the Heart

I was in Meijer's grocery store getting ready to fill my list
When I felt something giving my pants' leg a loving embrace,
I looked down and there was this little girl with blonde hair
Holding on tight with a beautiful smile on her face

She looked at me with such sweet, sweet love
I knew then that she was an angel come down to bless my soul,
Oh the blessings that I received that day
As she lifted me out of my grieving deep dark hole

My grieving was of that
Of the absence from me of my loving wife,
O Lord, I will never forget that little angel
I will remember that day for the rest of my life

This little girl is the first angel I have ever seen
Her face showed that she had *Down syndrome*,
But her beautiful smile could light up the sky and soften the hardest
 heart of stone
I will remember her always till that day that *God* comes to take me home.

We were in another place and time
There were no other people anywhere around,
As that little angel kept those smiles coming from her heart with love
As I stood there spellbound on that sacred heavenly ground

As quickly as this all happened
It was all over and she was no longer there,
As she disappeared like vapor in the air

I see shopper-filled aisles again
And I'm sure they had been all the while that I was in that other world,
With that beautiful little girl angel
Who was blessed with blue eyes and blonde curls

She looked so young
Like maybe three years old,
She was not there to take but to give
God showed me that day that she had a heart of gold

She blessed me that day
A blessing that I had deep need of,
Of which I will cherish forever
That beautiful heart flowing within with outward love

She was there to give me all the love she could give,
I will never forget that little angel who hugged my leg that day
No! Not as long as upon this earth I live

(P.T.L) T.M.K 4-11-2019 Thursday

Jim Godard

Jim Godard
Was not only a good friend to my wife and me,
But he became, through holy matrimony with my cousin,
A part of our family tree

We had a lot of good times
Enjoying get-together,
Camping out and cooking over a camp fire
In all kinds of weather

We are going to miss *Jim*
As also will his family and friends,
But we take heart in knowing
That he has now joined hands with *Jesus,* and his wife, and son again

Death is not the end, my friend
And if you know *Jesus* as *Lord* and savior,
You will unite again with loved ones who have gone on before
And of that, according to the Bible, I am very, very sure

When the eyes close forever here on earth
They open immediately in heaven's glorious domain,
It is a day of sorrow for those we leave behind
But for *Jim* it is a day of singing praises to *Jesus's* holy name

Death is not the end
It is the day that eternity begins,
It is the day of victory in *Jesus*
It is that day of rejoicing without end

Friends, relatives, and acquaintances
I pray that none of you, when your time comes, will be left behind,
Jesus is holding out his nail-pierced hands
To welcome you home when you cross that finish line

P.T.L #1662 4-2-2019

The Glory of a Wondering Star

Is there something missing in your life
And you know not what it is,
Reach out and grab the Bible
For inside are the answers that only *God* can give

He will direct your paths
He will keep you on the straight and narrow,
He will watch over you and guide you
As the songs in your heart begin to flow

Come to the altar of grace
Where the dark side will be cast away,
As you ask *Jesus* into your heart
Life will begin all over again with a brand new start

He will wash you clean
In the cleansing flow of the blood of the cross,
You will walk in the footsteps of *Jesus*
No more to walk this dark world with the lost

He will bless you with a gift in your heart
Of which to serve him,
He will lift you up and cast away all past sin
From that life of where you've been

He will guide you
As he blesses you wherever that you go,
As the beautiful songs within your heart
Begin to outward flow

Saving grace
Oh what beautiful words these are,
As you walk out of the darkness and into the light
Light like *Jesus's* birth and the glory of that wondering star

P.T.L. #1663 4-2-2019 *Tuesday*

From the Depths of My Heart

He keeps me from falling
He guides me all day long,
This is my calling
This is my song

He reached down and touched me
He opened my heart and created it new,
He gave me a beautiful gift to serve him
O *Lord,* from the depths of my heart I thank you

O how I love this gift of verse
Of bringing these words of hope and love to life,
And I also praise my father *God* for the gift of his son
My *Lord* and savior *Jesus Christ*

You picked me up when I was down
And set me up on higher ground,
No other blessings in life are greater
Than that which in *Jesus* I have found

O words of verse keep on coming
With blessings to my heart and my sisters and brothers,
I will write as long as I am able
And share my *God* of saving grace with others

Keep on flowing, oh wonderful gift
Let the messages be heard,
As I write and fight the good fight
Sharing *God's* gift to me of the living word

Praises keep flowing out from my pen
I pray that they never cease,
As they bless my heart and others
From the greatest on high to the lowest of the least

P.T.L. #1664 4-2-2019

Stoke the Fire

May the gospel of *Jesus Christ*
Spread like wild fire,
And may those flames shoot up
Rising higher, and higher, and higher

Get on fire for *Christ*
Spread the word near and far,
Spread it like butter on bread
Here, there, and everywhere like candy in a jar

We are *God's* messengers
Sharing of which is to come,
We are to reach out to others with *Jesus*
Before our days on earth are done

Be a vessel of honor to *Christ's* glory
Become a shining light,
Casting out the demons of darkness
Of the evil ones of the night

Shine on, oh Christian soldiers
Let the light of *Jesus* within shine out,
Sharing the love of *Jesus*
To draw them in to give the victory shout

Stoke the fire
And watch the flames rise
Let the dying embers
Rise up and fill the sky

Reach out, oh Christian soldier
And turn darkness into day,
Let the light of *Jesus* within you flow out
As you share him all along life's way

P.T.L. #1665 4-2-2019

The Altar of Grace

God loves me and blesses me.
And *God* will never leave me nor forsake me,
Oh what a wonderful promise
From my *God* who took upon himself my sins upon that tree

Miracles are still happening in my life
And I hold dear to those of the future, of those now, and of those
  that are past,
He has blessed me over and over again
For his help all we need to do is ask

God is always there
To listen to our prayers,
There to answer them
Because he really truly cares

God has promised to never leave us
He has promised to always be there,
We put our love and trust
Into the *Lord* of heaven's gentle care

If you have never given your heart to *Christ*
Find an altar of grace,
Invite *Jesus* to come into your heart
And rejoice for that better future that you now face

Oh what joy fills the converted heart
With blessings beyond belief,
Do not put off your salvation another day
Reach out and experience in *Jesus* the fullness of sin's release

Life will take on a whole new meaning
As you reach out and touch others around you,
God's blessings will pour out upon you
In all in his name that you undertake to say and do

P.T.L #1666 #1667 4-6-2019 (*I do not like those three sixes.*)

Goose Bumps and Tears of Joy

The world becomes a whole different place
When *God* comes to live within you,
Miracles will happen throughout your life
As angels appear with heavenly blessings of not a few

Nothing is impossible with *God*
I have experienced many a miracle,
Some with others and some alone
But the one I remember best is that of a little girl

She was an angel
Come down to bless me,
She had locked her arms around my leg
Just below the knee

She gave that leg a loving hug
And she looked up with a smile so beautiful,
Tears of joy began to moisten my eyes
As goose bumps jumped up and down covering my body to the full

Oh what wonderful joy she gave to me
Joy that I shall forever hold dear to my heart,
I will never forget that day as long as I live
I never wanted those little arms to ever from me depart

This is only one
Of the miracles to me that *God* has given,
Jesus's blessings just continue to flow
And I pray that they just keep coming as long as I am living

Life in *Jesus*
Is so beautiful,
When you live your life serving him
As you give your all to him, to the full

P.T.L. #1668 4-6-2019 *Saturday*

The Mission

Open up your heart's door
This you must do,
For it only opens from the inside out
Jesus has done his part and now you must do yours too

Open up the Bible
And read the words scrolled across its pages,
As its soul saving power touches your heart to bless others
As it always has and always will down through the ages

Words of life
Uplifting words,
Living words that leap up off the pages
To be reverently read and with listening ears heard

A word fitly spoken
Can soften the coldest hardest heart,
Along with a smile or a caress
As you with love do your *God*-given part

Christ showed us love—
We need to do to others no less,
We are in *Jesus's* name
To give our all of our very best

Dear sisters and brothers in *Christ*
Continue to use your gifts that *God* has given to you,
Don't hold back, don't be slack
And *God* will bless all in his name that you undertake to do

Love conquers all obstacles and fears
God's love for us is beyond comprehension,
The cross is the greatest love story ever written
It is where *Christ* filled to the full his earthly mission

P.T.L #16694-8-2019

Songs of Praise of Endless Days

Hallelue What a Savior

I'm ready to trade in those songs
That I sing over here that are so beautiful and fair,
For those songs far more joyous
That awaits us to be sung over there

Praises to *Jesus* shall never cease
Glory to *God* we will sing on high,
As we become clothed in shining white
And crowned in gold in that ivory home beyond the sky

With angels all around us
We will sing those old familiar hymns,
And the new ones, oh so heavenly
As we praise our *Lord* and *Savior* with those flowing out from within

Through the *Holy Spirit*
He lives with us and in us,
He fills us with so much love
We feel like we could bust

Jesus is here
And *Jesus* is there,
The *God* of heaven and earth
Is everywhere

We look forward to that day
To be forever with him and our loved ones,
As we lift up our voice and rejoice kneeling before *God's* throne
When our days on earth are over and done

And oh how I desire to meet
That little blue-eyed, blonde angel again,
I not only love her for the angel that she is
But as a close and dearest to my heart friend

Amen Hallelue

P.T.L. #1670 4-9-2019 *Tuesday*

The Book of Life

What's inside of me must come out
And put on paper with ink and pen,
What *God* gives to me I want to share with my sisters and brothers
And to draw those of the wayward souls in

Touch those that walk in darkness
Dear *God,* let your blessings flow,
Draw them into the light
That they may be cleansed and glistening like flakes of shiny snow

The end for each of us
Of our days on earth are coming,
If you are in a marathon race for *Jesus*
Keep those feet shod and running

Jesus is coming back one day
To lift us up to him,
Are you reaching out to draw others in?

We all have a Christian duty
To reach the lost before our days on earth come to an end,
Do you share your gifts and Christian love with others?
Of strangers and of friends

We need to spread the salvation message
The book of life is open,
Wouldn't you like for *Jesus*
To sign your name on those pages therein?

If your name is not in the book of life
It will be found in those who are destined for the lake of fire,
Where never ending flames rise up like a volcano
Shooting up higher and higher

P.T.L. #1671 4-9-2019

Behind Closed Doors

I try to put it sweetly
And oh so very completely,
Of what lies beyond this world
For you, and others, and me

What we do here on earth
Will follow us into eternity,
Good or bad, rejoicing or tears so sad
Chained to sin's destiny or in *Jesus* forever set free

Life gives us many choices
What we do here determines our final destiny,
Are you walking on the dark side?
Or in the light of *Jesus* set free

Choices
Choose you this day who you will serve,
Will it be that fallen angel of hell's domain?
Or the one who of your sins is the only cure

Reach out, *God* is only a prayer away
He will change your life and destiny,
His shed blood will wash all your sins away

He is a loving *God*
Waiting for souls to invite him in,
And believe me
Heaven is far greater than the devil's den

He opens the door
That no man can shut,
And he closes the doors of the past
To never be again opened up

P.T.L. #1672 4-8-2019 *Tuesday*

Up or Down

I do not know what to do
I have no close friends,
But I do have the gift of verse
And a few pencils and pens

Poems of verse are my calling
Beautiful uplifting poems of heavenly light,
Whatever the seed that my *Lord* gives to me
I plant and it grows to a full bloom like a beautiful flower oh so brilliantly bright

These poems were written to speak to the hearts of others
With a gentle and caring voice,
I try to let others know
Of *Jesus* and the devil and that they have a choice

Christ does not enter in
Where he is not wanted,
He enters only to those who ask of him
To cleanse them of their sin

Death is not discriminating
It comes to each and every one,
You can either go down to be with the devil and the fallen angels
Or go up to be with *God's Son*

The easiest way to hell is to do absolutely nothing
Heaven's gate will only open,
For those who have opened their heart's door
To invite the *Lord* of life to come in

Take *Jesus* as your *Lord* and *Savior*
And don't go anywhere near the devil's den again,
And *Jesus* will bless you beyond measure
And take you one day to live forever with him

P.T.L. #1673 4-10-2019 *Wednesday*

The Angel Came Down from Heaven

On the day of the twenty-ninth of March two thousand and nineteen
I went to *Meijers* grocery store,
And something wonderfully amazing happened
As soon as I walked through that door

I had entered into another time and place
I felt something wrap tightly around my leg just below my knee,
I felt the tug get tighter
As I reached down to release whatever was gripping me

And as I looked down
There was a little girl angel looking back up at me,
With a face glowing bright and shining
She was holding on tight not wanting to release her grip and set me free

She showed no fear
As she continued giving me her beautiful smile,
And I looked around and there was no one else to be found
Except a young lady angel just across the aisle

We were in another place and time
There were no other people anywhere around,
As that little angel kept those smiles coming from her heart with love
As I stood there spellbound on that sacred heavenly ground

Then I looked around
And they were nowhere to be seen,
I stood there fully aware that everything was back to normal
And I know without a doubt this was not a dream

I see shopper-filled aisles again
And I'm sure they had been all the while that I was in that other world,
With that beautiful little girl angel
Blessed with blue eyes and blonde curls

She blessed me that day
A blessing that I had deep need of,
Of which I will cherish forever
That beautiful heart flowing within with outward love

She had the face of *Down syndrome*
She had a loving heart that outward to me was shown,
She blessed my soul to the full that day
With greater love than I have ever known

P.T.L. #1672 4-11-2019 *Thursday*

The Sacrificial Lamb

Good Friday
Is that dark day that *Jesus* was crucified on the cross,
Easter Sunday is that day that he arose triumphant over death and the grave
And with nail-pierced hands and saving grace he's reaching out through us to reach the lost

We are to do what he has blessed us to do
We are to be touching hearts to be won,
And the only cure for the condemnation of sin
Is the blood of the sacrificial lamb, our *Father God's* only begotten son

It was for us that he gave his all
To him our lives we owe,
We need to reach out to those around us
With the way of salvation through *Jesus* wherever that we go

He is the living waters
Reaching out to those who are athirst,
He's coming back for all
All those who came in last and all who came in first

Jesus does not discriminate
Of color, nationality, gender, nor race,
He's coming back for those who are now saved
To raise them up and usher them through that pearly gate

Rejoice o' *Christian* soldiers
Eternity is only one last breath away,
It could be tomorrow, next week, or next year
But it could be today

Don't you hear *Jesus* calling you?
Come home oh wondering soul,
And make, on earth, before death takes hold
Heaven, your final destiny, as your goal

P.T.L. #1757 4-15-2019 *Monday*

Of Snowflakes and Angels

When *God's*
love flowed over my soul,
It was my heart
That he stole

He gave me a gift that day
With which to love and serve him,
A gift of poems of light
To write down on paper with ink and pen

When I see the sunrise and the sunsets
I see my *Jesus*,
And when the refreshing showers of spring arrives
I see my *Jesus*

As I gaze in awe and admiration
Of the colored leaves of fall,
I ponder upon all the beauty of his creation
Rejoicing for the wonder of it all

When I see the snowflakes of winter
Of oh so brilliant treasures sparkling like diamonds in the pale moonlight,
I think of that day when *Jesus* and all the holy angels fill the sky
As they come to lift us up into heaven's never fading light

When souls reach out to *Jesus*
They will experience one of many more miracles happening,
I can almost hear the angels singing
Glory in the highest to our *Lord God*, creator of every thing

All of converted hearts shall burst forth in song
Singing glory to *God* for the *Holy Spirit* came down to make his bode in us,
And filled with showers of blessings from above
That one day we will forever abode in heaven with our *Lord* and savior *Jesus*

P.T.L. #1676, 4-18-2019 *Thursday*

The Family of God

We live in a dark world
I hunger for the next,
I gave my heart to *Jesus*
Who gives to me his best

He gives each of us a gift in which to serve him
A gift to share with others,
He gave us each a new heart to reach out with Christian love
To share with the lost and one another

We each and every one
Need lifting up every now and then,
We need love from our Christian sisters and brothers
And our dear and close friends

We need to reach out to those in darkness
And invite them to step out into the light,
And take a little walk with *Jesus*
And ask him to take away what's wrong and make it right

Ask him to change your life and your eternal destination
Ask him to change your heart,
Find an altar of grace
Is a good place to start

Ask him into your heart
And he will give you a new one to direct your path,
Love him and it will be reflected back to you
like all who have ever come to him now have

His love is eternal
His love is an everlasting one,
Christ will love you as a sister or a brother
And his father will love you like a daughter or a son

P.T.L. #1677 4-22-2019 *Monday*

Streets of Gold

God's love is internally, outwardly,
And eternal,
And sure beats the devil's fire infernal

Life is but a passing moment
And if you a *Christian* be,
Live life to the full sharing the love of *Jesus*
Who took upon himself our sins nailed to that tree

Use those gifts that *God* has given
Use them to draw others to the cross,
Witness to the world that's around you
With Christian love reach out to the lost

Lift up your Christian brothers and sister in Christ
Life for them is not always a bed of roses,
Sometimes their continence is down
And sometimes we too are one with those

Become a beacon of light
To all you meet along life's highways and byways,
And *Jesus* will pour out his blessings upon you
All the rest of your days

Let the love of *Jesus* within
Shine out all your life,
Sharing with others
Of the one who paid sin's price

Stay on the upward paths
Walk the straight and narrow road,
Live life to the full in *Jesus*
Knowing that one day you will walk those streets of gold

P.T.L. #1678 4-23-2019 *Tuesday*

Seek and Ye Shall Find

God has put a song in my heart
Oh if only I could sing,
My voice is like that of a croaking frog
And that is why poetry is now my thing

God's gifts vary
But *God* is the giver of all that I know,
We cherish all those that he has given
As his blessings come pouring out like that of a rolling mighty river flow

When we use those gifts that *God* has given
His light comes shining through,
He loves us all, each and every one
Drawing in others through these gifts he's given to me and you

He is the light that outshines the sun
The light that guides us through the dark days,
He takes away our every shadow of doubt
As faith moves mountains to fade away

He is there for us every minute of every hour
As we should be every day for him,
He has promised to always be there for us
Through good times and all the trials of thick and thin

Jesus has promised to never leave nor forsake us
As we share our love and cares with him every given day,
In spirit and in flesh we serve our risen savior
Sharing his blessings to others along life's narrow way

Jesus is love
Jesus is life everlasting,
He is the *God* of miracles that awaits us all
As we in faith believe in the Bible's written words of everything

P.T.L #1679 4-30-2019 *Tuesday*

O Lord, Let It Be, Oh Let It Be

One day at a time, sweet *Jesus*
One day at a time,
I am *Jesus's*
And *Jesus* is mine

He went to the cross for me
He gave his life to set me free,
My life is his to do with what he will
O *Lord* let it be, oh let it be

I walk the line
I serve a risen savior,
Wherever he leads I will follow
The blood of *Jesus* cleanses me clean and pure

I walk the straight and narrow
Sharing the creator of the heavens and the earth,
The *Lord God* of heaven
The holy child of the virgin birth

His love flows over every soul
Every soul who opens their heart to invite him in,
He washes them clean of all their past
Of all wherever they've been

One day at a time, sweet *Jesus*
We live the new life you gave to us,
To share your love with others
And this is what we must

We are saved
To bring honor to our *Lord*,
Saved to use the gifts that he has given to you and me
O *Lord* let it be, oh let it be

P.T.L. #1680 5-1-2019 *Wednesday*

The Pearly Gates

Keep your heart and mind on *Jesus*
And not on the things that will lead you astray,
And his blessings will bring comfort to your soul
As he keeps your heart from drifting away

What a wonderful *Lord* and *Savior*
Filled with love greater than we have ever known,
We will reap of his treasures one day, oh glorious day
From the blessings to others on earth that we have sown

If you desire treasures most precious
More precious than silver and gold,
Give your heart and soul to *Jesus*
And watch his treasures before you unfold

Souls reaching out to *Jesus*
Drawn in from testimonials that touched their heart,
We each have gifts to share with others
As *God* lays his blessings upon us as we do our part

Life is so beautifully heart warming
When you know *Jesus* as *Lord* and savior,
Let your blessings flow down, dear *Lord*
Like springtime's life-giving rainy days of weather

God is the only one who can change lives
And he blesses us as we do our part,
It is a beautiful cycle of conversions of hearts and souls
As we share our *Jesus* with others out of a loving heart

Jesus has given us deep love for those who are lost
And a desire to make our world a better place,
As we reach out to draw others into the arms of *Jesus*
That they may go one day rejoicing into those open pearly gates

P.T.L. #1681 5-2-2019 *Thursday*

The Road Less Traveled

When wisdom abides in the heart of man
God will guide his footsteps,
He will not want or lack
In following *God* his integrity shall be kept

He shall never fail *God*
And *God* shall never fail him,
As he walks the paths of righteousness
Far from the pathways of sin

His heart door is open
Blessed by *God* both pure and clean,
To let the light of heaven within shine out
As he lives forever trusting in *God* to lean

Righteousness fills his soul
As he makes serving *God* his lifetime goal

No other paths will he walk
Only those that *God* has set before him,
He walks the paths of righteousness
With a heart filled with *God's* love within

He walks the narrow road
He reaches out to those that are burdened with a heavy load

God is his guide through life
His footsteps are upon the straight and narrow,
He follows where *God* leads
Every day and every tomorrow

He will not alter his steps
As he follows that less traveled road,
He goes where *God* leads him to go
That others may receive *God's* love to forever have and to hold

P.T.L #1682 5-3-2019 *Friday*

Our Father God's Only Begotten Son

Open up my heart's door, dear *Father God*
That all may see,
Your son *Jesus*
Living inside of me

And open up the hearts of others
That they too may know,
The wonderful blessings of *Jesus's* pure sweet love
To come into their hearts and outward to others flow

Jesus is only a prayer away,
Won't you reach out to him today?

And know without a shadow of a doubt
That when your time on earth is done,
That you have a home in heaven
With *Father God's* only begotten son

He's waiting
Waiting for you to open up your heart's door,
And ask him to come in and cleanse your soul
That you may dwell with him one day forever and ever more

He will fill your soul with love
With his love to share with others,
As you become a vessel of shining light for him
A shining light to draw in new sisters and brothers

We will become farmers for *Jesus*
Making ready for that harvest to come,
That day that we rise up to an angel-filled sky
Greeted and welcomed home by our Father *God's* only begotten son

P.T.L. #1683 5-5-2019 *Sunday*

The Greatest Gift of All

Give me the words to write
To draw souls out of the darkness
And into the light

Lord, you took my wife from me
I know it's but for a little while,
For one day you will take that frown from my face
And replace it with a smile

There is not a day goes by
That my thoughts stray from my wife's absence from me,
I want to go home to be with the love of my life
And from this cruel world to be set free

May all obstacles before me
Be taken out of my path,
That I may be filled to the full
With all the blessings for me that you have

O Holy Spirit
Give me souls to seek,
Fill me with love for others
And give me the words to speak

I need a greater purpose
To live to the full my life,
A greater purpose for living
And I know that it can only be found in *Christ*

Put my feet on higher ground
Lead me on the path that I should walk,
Give me a heart for others
And the encouraging words to live and to talk

May the *God* of all creation
Put a smile upon your face,
Open up your heart and invite him in
And receive his greatest gift of all, of amazing, amazing grace

P.T.L. #1684 5-13-2019 *Monday*

Open Your Heart's Door

With open arms
Jesus is waiting to welcome us home,
And for all those who have lost loved ones
With *Jesus* they will never again know the sorrow of being alone

Filled with joy and unending glory
They will unite with loved ones again,
Surrounded by angels rejoicing for the victory that they have won
Singing glory to *God* our Lord and savior, amen and amen

Jesus's promises
Are locked in steadfast and sure,
And the blood that was shed on that old rugged cross
Is our *Father God's* gift to us of reconciliation, sin's only cure

Where he leads we are to follow,
Not only today
But of all of our every tomorrow

His love has become forever mine,
No greater love could I ever come to know nor ever hope to find

Do you know *Jesus* as *Lord* and savior, are you ready for judgment day?
Have you been to the altar of grace?
Believe and reach out for there is no other way

He died to set souls free he died out of his love for the lost,
He came to reconcile fallen man back to our *Father God* again
Through his blood that was shed upon the cross

He took our sins upon himself
You have to reach out for redemption to receive,
Faith is the substance of things hoped for
With unwavering faith, this you must believe

You only, have the key to your heart
Only you can open your heart's door and let the *Lord* of life in,
Only the shed blood of *Jesus* on the cross can wash your sins away
This you must know, that salvation comes only through him

P.T.L. #1685 5-23-2019 *Thursday*

Glistening like Gold

We each have a duty to do
And we each have our own way of doing it,
God has given us life to be lived to the full
And a heart of love to reach out with

Lighten the world around you
Use those gifts that *God* has given,
I envy those who can sing and dance
As they use those gifts for *Jesus* all their rest of days of living

And those who can pluck the strings of a guitar
And also all those who can master the piano and its ivory keys,
Souls reaching out and touching others with beautiful music
And those who pray daily down on bended knee

We all have been given something
Of which to honor our blessed savior,
Something to reach out with to draw others in
With love and affection flowing out of clean and pure

Oh how we love to praise *Jesus*
With those old timey religion's precious hymns,
With love we shake the rafters as we sing
Joyfully rattling the windows from within

Praises, oh so beautiful precious praises
In honor lifted up to him,
As those songs come forth echoing from the heart
Lifting up on and on all the way to the heaven of heavens

Our praises will never cease here on earth
From the hearts of the redeemed,
Neither of that which is now nor of that which is yet to come
As we one day rise to glory glowing like gold through the clouds
Like beautiful upward sunbeams

P.T.L. #1686 5-25-2019 *Saturday*

No Greater Love

Keep your heart and mind on *Jesus*
And not on things that will lead you away,
And his blessings will bring comfort to your soul
And keep you from going astray

What a wonderful savior is ours
With love greater than we have ever known,
As we reap of the treasures
Of the gospel message that we have to others sown

Touching souls and hearts
To reach out to the creator of heaven and earth,
To *Jesus Christ,* the *Son* of *God*
Praying that others may experience the miracle of rebirth

Come and be filled with the *Holy Spirit*
Come and be filled with his gifts from above,
Gifts to reach out to touch others
With *God's* saving grace purchased on the cross for us with love

A love so perfect, a love so wonderful we scarce can take it in
That our *Father God* would offer up his son,
For a sacrifice for our sin
Won't you reach out and open your heart
And invite the *Lord* of life to come in?

No greater love could you ever know
No greater love could *God* ever give,
Than that cross of Calvary and his son
Where *Christ* died that all through faith may forever live

Reach out
He is but a prayer away,
Waiting for you to come to him
And to live with him in his heavenly home of eternal day

P.T.L. #1687 5-27-2019 *Monday*

New Heavens and a New Earth

There is a place
Of tranquil peace,
A heavenly place
Of sweet release

Where all the burdens of life
Fade away,
In the light of our savior
In that home of eternal day

When our time on earth
Comes to an end,
He will welcome us home
To live forever with him

Oh what a wonderful savior
A wonderful savior is he,
Who died on the cross
And rose to life again to set us free

Death is not the end, my friend
For when our eyes close and our days on earth are over and done,
We will open them to the rejoicing of angels
And to our long ago departed loved ones
And most of all our *Father God's* only begotten *Son*

We whose names
Are written in the *Lamb's* book of life need never to fear,
For *Christ* promised to never leave nor forsake us
As we look forward to that day that he draws near

The devil one day and all his followers
Will get their just due,
As they wallow forever in that lake of fire
As we thank *Jesus* for the new heavens and new earth
That he created for me and you

P.T.L. #1688 5-30-2019 *Thursday*

Father's Day

We have our dads that we call father
And we honor them on this Father's day,
And when we became one with *Jesus*
A new father became ours that day

Jesus became our brother
And *God* became our heavenly *Father* both to me and to you
It's hard to explain this in words
But the Bible states of this to be absolutely true

A new heart is placed within us
As we are washed clean in *Christ's* blood,
As *God's* mercy washes over us
Like a cleansing flood

Yes! This is Father's day
The day that we honor our paternal fathers,
As also we lift our songs and praises
To our heavenly *Father* and his *Son's* shed blood
That flows over us like cleansing living waters

We praise our heavenly *Father* this day
Along with our paternal fathers too,
We cherish them both with all that we are
And in everything that we do

Happy Father's day to all
I pray that the songs and poems lifted you up this day,
And for you and every one of fathers
We pray *God's* blessing continue to come your way

P.T.L #1689 6-11-2019 Tuesday

Life and Death

I miss my grandpa, and grandma, and my mother, and dad
And all my uncles, and aunts, and my cousins too,
And I lost my wife, the love of my life
And now my fear is that my children will pass on before I do

I pray daily for their health and welfare
And that they know *Jesus* as *Lord* and *Savior*,
And each one is ready when their life on earth comes to an end
Making sure that their heart is clean and pure

I pray that you don't leave this world
Before I do,
It would break my heart
For I love with all my heart each and every one of you

I will continue to pray for my children
And I know that *God* listens and answers prayers,
He is the light that shines in my heart
And I pray that he is also the light in theirs

My children have shown me so much love
And I pray that my love comes shining back to them,
I love you each and every one
As I hold you dear in my heart within

I pray for each one of you
And that you continue that closer walk with *Jesus*,
And the bond of love of you and me
Always be filled between us

Life is short
And no matter when life here on earth comes to an end,
With *Jesus* one day
We will all be reunited together again

P.T.L #1691 6-13-2019 *Thursday*

The Awe and Wonder of It All

I looked out my bedroom window
And into the blackness of the night,
And there in the shadows amongst the trees
Were lightning bugs blinking with sparkles of golden light

I heard what sounded like base drums down in the swamp land
As the big bullfrogs added their special music to the fray,
And I heard the birds' sweet songs floating freely in the air
As the sun peaked over the eastern horizon turning the night into day

Carp were splashing everywhere all around the lake
Casting out upon the weeds and the moss their belly filled with eggs,
As all around them on half sunken logs
Turtles were basking in the morning sun with outstretched legs

I heard a morning dove cooing for rain
And a black bird singing as he roosted on top of a cattail,
I heard the screech of a hawk and a blue heron's squawk
And I see buzzards down yonder on a fence rail

Flowers were blooming everywhere
With colors of yellow, white, and blue,
And all around the shaggy sagging bark of the dead elm trees
Upon the ground golden yellow and grey morels were bursting through

As each season pours out its beauty before our eyes
We look on in awe of the wonders of it all,
As we in wondrous joy bask in each season's glory
Of spring, summer, winter, and fall

And when we gaze upon these seasons of differing awesome beauty
That wonderfully is spread out before us,
We praise the one who created the all of everything
Our *Lord God* of heaven and earth, *Christ Jesus*

P.T.L. #1691 6-30-2019 *Sunday*

Beyond the Portals of Death

Death befalls us all
To each and every one as we take that last breath,
And walk through that dark valley
That dark valley of death

For Christians, we each and every one
A light will appear out of the darkness,
As we walk that pathway that leads upward into heaven
And into the arms of *Jesus* and his loving welcoming caress

Death is not the end my friend
It is only the beginning,
Heaven is there waiting for all who have opened their heart to invite
 him in
It is our home of a beautiful place without end

Christian brothers and sisters
O what joy awaits us all,
Every repentant soul
Who has answered the Holy Spirit's call

We will encounter angels on high rejoicing
Singing the victory song,
As we are ushered into heaven
Where the past is forever forgotten and gone

Along with the saved and the holy angels
We will continue to praise *Jesus* forever and forever more,
Basking in the blessings of heaven and all of its glorious light and wonders
Where we will be welcomed home as we walk through those pearly gates' open doors

Yes! Life is not the end my friend
Life after death is just the beginning,
It is a time and place to dwell with *Jesus* and the holy *angels*, and our loved ones once again
Forever in a paradise that has no beginning and no ending

P.T.L. #1692 7-4-2019 *Wednesday*

Praise the *Lord!*

Cling to His Promises

Keep your eyes on the path
Turn not to the left or to the right,
When darkness begins to surround you
Continue going toward the light

There are many temptations in this world
To draw you into sin,
When the devil attempts to lure you away
Look to the Lord of heaven and keep your eyes on him

The world, the lust of the eyes, and the lust of the flesh
Bears three of the most deadly sins,
And the pride of life added on
Makes one more of Satan's ploys to lure you in

When temptations come your way
Pray to *Jesus* to remove them from your heart,
As you walk the straight and narrow
Clinging to his promise to never from you depart

Walk in the light of *Jesus*
With every step that you take,
Ask *Christ* to guide you through life
And place your trust in him for every decision that you make

He has promised
To never leave nor forsake you,
You need to promise him the same
And fulfill that promise with all you say and do

Love flows freely both ways my friend
From us to him and from him to us,
As we give our heart and soul to the one
Whose shed blood for our sins we have come to trust

P.T.L. #1693 7-11-2019 *Thursday*

The Sweet, Sweet By-and-By

Angels on high singing
As we sing along with those who have gone on before,
Oh for the beauty that will surround us
As we set foot upon that far off distant shore

What wonders await us
When our life here on earth passes us by,
As we receive our father *God's* welcome to our heavenly home,
Our home in that promised land that lies beyond the sky

Sins forgiven and forgotten
Never again to be looked back upon,
As we rejoice with loved ones who have gone on before
Shouting hallelujahs for the victory that we have won

Joy, oh what joy
Joy for every repented soul,
Who lived their life to the full serving *Jesus*
Making that their lifetime purpose and goal

We are here but for a moment
Compared to the eons of endless time,
In that place that lies on that far off distant shore
Where we will shout the victory cry as we pass over the line

Sing glory to the holy trinity of *Holy Ghost, Jesus,*
And our *Father God* who reigns on high,
Where the victory shouts ring out forever
In that awesome place of *God's* sweet, sweet by-and-by

P.T.L. #1694 7-23-2019 *Tuesday*

Sharing the Love

More about *Jesus* we desire
Deep down in our hearts to know,
More about *Jesus*
We desire in him to continually grow

Jesus you are our all
You are our all of everything,
Our hearts continually yearn to be forever with you
And to join in with the angels and the spiritual songs that they sing

I know that in heaven
We will know as we are known,
With no remembrance of our past life
Of any and all failings that we have ever sown

You've touched our hearts, *Lord*
In so many miraculous and loving ways,
You have blessed us over and over
All through the trials of all our earthly days

The love that you have for us
Is like no other love that we shall ever know,
And of all our days of life on earth
We will continue to share that love everywhere of wherever that we go

P.T.L. #1695 7-30-2019 *Tuesday*

Riches Untold

We may not be rich here on earth
But if we know *Jesus* as our savior and Lord,
We will rise up one day rejoicing
As we receive our eternal reward

His love here on earth
Will see us through,
As we give him the praise
In all that we say and do

We are here
But for a little while,
As we share our *Jesus* with others
With loving care and a smile as we go that extra mile

He is there with us
Every step of the way,
As we walk and talk with him
Throughout our every *God*-given day

No matter what life throws our way
We always look forward to the prize,
Of that that lies beyond this world
There in heaven's glistening golden streets and crystal clear skies

Jesus's love for us
With his shed blood alone,
Proved to us on the cross
That his love is greater than any that we have ever known

Oh for that joy that awaits us
When we cross over to that other side,
To be forever with our risen savior
And our loved ones to forever and ever abide

P.T.L. #1696 8-1-2019 *Thursday*

The Gift of Verse

I've got jiggers
And I've got fleas,
And I've got bow legs
And knobby knees

I've got a lazy eye
Amongst other things
And a croaking voice
And that for sure proves to me that I cannot sing

There are many things that I do not have or can do
But with the gift of verse I have been blessed
Of rhyming words all filled in together
I don't need all the rest

I know that what I have
Is *God's* special gift to me,
And I am going to keep on writing
Right on into eternity

I love my Lord and he loves me
What else could anyone ask for?
I will follow wherever that he leads
From sea to shining sea to that far off shore

He has given me a course to walk
A path upon the earth to follow,
With not only words written on paper
But words to live by every day and every tomorrow

You have given me more love, dear *Lord*
Than this mortal body can hold within,
I have been born again to share that love with others
Through these poems that continue to flow through my pen

P.T.L. #1697 8-1-2019 *Thursday*

Open Your Heart's Door

Yesterday is but a shadow of things yet to come
What we do today determines our eternal destiny,
We must live life to the full in our risen savior
With all within us we place our trust, O *Lord*, in thee

Jesus has given us a greater purpose for living
With all that he has planted within our heart,
We are to reach out to others to share his blessings of eternal light
Rejoicing as for him we do our part

We praise you, O *Lord*, for your presence within us
And for your gift to us of a new heart,
With which to draw others in
O *Lord God* of heaven and earth how great thou art

With those gifts that you have blessed us with to serve you
We pray to share your love with others,
With music flowing from our heart and soul
We pray to gain for you, *Lord*, new sisters and new brothers

With your promise to us of a home beyond the sky
Of that heavenly realm of a better place,
We praise your holy name
And thank you for your gift of amazing, oh amazing grace

You have ignited our souls
With your unquenchable flames of heavenly light,
That we may shine out and share with others
Like the stars in the heavens that brighten the darkness of the night

With love beyond all comprehension
You've shed your blood to wash away our sin,
Giving eternal life to all who open their hearts
And invite you to forever come and dwell within

P.T.L #1698 8-21-2019 *Wednesday*

Where Rejoicing Shall Never Cease

This world is a proving ground of *Satan's* domain
Of where we must serve *Jesus* faithfully in all we say and do,
First we must open our heart's door and invite *Jesus* in
Then be always to him faithful and true

We must ask *Jesus* to guide us through this life
And to bless our souls now and forever,
As we share his love with our sisters and brothers in *Christ*
In a church every Sunday as we gather together

What a wonderful life waits all who are born again
Both now and when we depart from this world,
As we reunite again with our departed loved ones
To be welcomed home by the holy *God* of the living word

Oh to be able to see *Jesus* in all his majesty and glory
And to sing with all his faithful angels above,
As we shed tears of joy with our loved ones
Rejoicing as we gather together with them again with love

Joy, oh endless joy
Given to all who have come to him,
Oh what wonderful joy flows through our hearts
Of the holy *Lord God* of heaven who took upon himself our condemnation of sin

Jesus's creation of the new heavens and the new earth
Is to be our new home forevermore filled with joy and peace,
With sweet music floating freely everywhere
Of songs of joyful praises lifted up to *Jesus* of which will never cease

O holy *Lord God* of all creation
Who took upon himself all our burdens to bear,
We will praise you for all eternity and beyond
For opening the gates of heaven to greet us with open arms and loving care

P.T.L. #1699 8-30-2019 8-31-2019 *Saturday*

There Is No Other Way

O holy *Lord God* of heaven and earth
O how I love to spread your fame,
Born again to spread the holy gospel's truth
In honor of your holy name

You are the *God* of all creation
The holy *God* of heaven and earth,
You are the one and only *God*
Who by the *Holy Ghost* and the *Virgin Mary* became a man child of
    holy birth

You came to reconcile all who reach out
Back to the *Father* again,
Through the gift of the grace of *God*
We all now have the opportunity to be born again

Jesus through that old rugged cross opened the gates of heaven,
To usher in all who would come to him
To be cleansed by his blood that washes away all sin

There is no other way
Won't you give your heart to *Jesus* today?
Life here on earth will come to an end we know not when
Procrastination could put your soul in harm's way

There is no greater joy in life
Than knowing that one day you will be with *Jesus*,
Far from the depths of hell and suffering
And all the evil that abounds on this earth around us

P.T.L. #1700 8-30-2019 *Friday*

It's Our Turn

Lead us, *Lord*, in the paths of righteousness
Guide us through every step,
Place your words of love in our hearts
To share with others of the one who paid our debt

The desire within our soul
Is to be a vessel of honor, O *Lord God*, for you,
Reaching out to share with others
Your messages of oh so faithful and true

Jesus is the one and only
True and faithful *God* with a capital G,
Jesus and his shed blood
Is the only cure for sin, for you and me

Come to him in undying faith
And watch your faith move the mountains,
God will give you a new and wonderful outlook on life
As you are washed in the cleansing blood of *Christ's* ever flowing fountain

Get baptized
Receive with joy an everlasting brand new heart,
To never look back again upon the sins of the past
Come and be born again with sins forgiven and forgotten and a brand new life to start

Step out into the light
Walk *God's* paths of the straight and narrow,
Absorb in your heart *God's* life-giving words that are written down on the Bible's pages
Sharing with others of *God's* love in your every day and your every tomorrow

Jesus reached out
To draw us to him,
Now it is our turn, of those of us who are saved
To do our part to draw others in

P.T.L. #1701 9-12-2019 *Thursday*

Out of the Darkness

If you don't have *Jesus*
When your life comes to an end,
You will spend eternity
In outer darkness, my friend

Into the fires of hell
With never a moment of relief,
Forever is a long time
For all who never came to believe

Don't leave this world
Without *Jesus* by your side,
It was for your salvation
That on that cruel cross he died

The blood of *Christ* that was shed on the cross
Is the only thing that can cleanse you of your sin,
First of all you must repent then open your heart's door
Then invite the *Lord* of life to come in

Do not face eternity
Without *Jesus* my friend,
For that dark side is forever
Forever without end

I was forty years old
Before I saw the light,
I opened the Bible for the first time
And the light of day overcame the dark of the night

As long as you have the breath of life
The door of heaven can open to let you in,
But first you must open your heart's door
And ask the *Lord* of life to wash away your sin

P.T.L. #1702 9-12-2019 *Thursday*

All the Way to the Promised Land

My *Jesus*, my *Jesus*
O *Lord*, you are my holy *Jesus*,
Oh Christian sisters and brothers
Jesus has promised always to be there for us

Through the good times and the bad
God is with us wherever that we are,
To rejoice with us when we are happy and to lift us up when we are down and sad

Why would you want to face your trials alone?
When you can have *Jesus* by your side,
Open up your heart to the *Lord God* of glory
And experience a love of far greater heights and endless blessings of wide

He promised that he would always be there for us
Life becomes more worth the living,
When we quit spending our lives getting
And start spending it in giving

Life in *Jesus*
Is more precious than silver and gold,
No greater treasure could one ever find to have and to hold
Than those in the holy Bible of those sacred words of blessings of old

Jesus is the answer
To every question to ever be asked,
He is the *God* of all creation
And he is the one who took upon himself our every sin of the past

He promised when we came to him to walk with us
And be our guide all the way to the promised land,
Won't you reach out to him with unwavering love, faith, and hope?
The one who took upon himself for our sins the cross and his nail-pierced feet and hands

P.T.L. #1703 9-20-2019 *Friday*

Oh for the Joy of That Which Awaits Us

I loved that lady
My heart with love to overflowing she did fill,
What do I mean I loved that lady?
I love that lady and I always will

Alice was the sunshine of my life
She filled my soul with everlasting love,
And one day, oh glorious day, I will be with her again
In that heavenly home above

"*In the Garden*" sweet *Alice*
We will sing that song again,
In that beautiful home in heaven
Where eternal love with *Jesus* will never end

Oh what joy awaits us all
All who have given their hearts to him,
Where music floats freely in the air
Where eternal life begins without end

We will bask in the love of *Jesus*
We will sing sweet songs with the angels,
We will caress our long ago passed love ones
As we hear the echoes of those long ago church bells

We will dance and sing praises
As we walk those golden streets,
Lifting our voices filled with the joy of *Jesus*
And to the music tapping our feet to its beats

Hallelujah what a savior
O what love flows to us through him,
O what a day like no other shall ever be
When we go to be forever with him

P.T.L. #1704 9-23-2019 *Monday*

Oh What a Day That Will Be

What *God* has given
We want to share with others,
Of the love that he has placed within us
In all our sisters and brothers

Jesus, Jesus, Jesus
Oh there is just something about that name,
That makes you want to shout for glory
To the one from heaven to earth he came

He came to open the gates of heaven
Through his blood that he shed upon the cross,
Shed to wash away the sins of all who come to him
To cleanse of those that are lost

Jesus Christ the *King* of *kings*
The almighty creator of all, of everything

There is no other fount I know
That can wash our sins away,
No other like that old rugged cross and that crimson flow
Cleansing us of that dark past to pure, and clean, and white as snow

Sins forgiven and forgotten
Never to be remembered again,
Names written down in the book of life
To one day meet *Jesus* and to raise up and dwell forever with him

As that old familiar song of
Oh what a day, oh what a day of rejoicing that will be,
When we all see *Jesus*
And sing and shout for the victory

P.T.L. #1705 9-23-2019 *Monday*

The Living Word

O *Lord God*, open our hearts
To absorb the heights and depths of the written word,
Bless us with searching eyes and minds
As we open up the Bible or when we go to church where those holy
    words are heard

We pray to understand of that which is now
And of that which is yet to come,
O *Father God* of heaven and earth
We pray for that closer walk with you and your only begotten son

Jesus has placed so much love in our hearts
And if ever in any way we have fallen back,
We must ask him for forgiveness
And of his unwavering love for us we will never lack

His love is wider and deeper
Than the ocean and the deep blue sea,
I know that none of us are perfect
But I also know that *Jesus* has made his abode in us for all to see

The desire of my life
Is to be a living testimony for him,
As I continue to write in verse of his love and compassion
With all in me that he has placed within

We love these life-changing living words of the Bible
Jesus is the living word,
He is the holy word that opens up searching hearts
To receive the invitation as it is either read or heard

For all who are saved
We have our Christian duties to perform,
So that others too may rise up to heaven one day
Crowned with a golden crown and with pure white coverings adorned

P.T.L. #1706 10-9-2019 *Wednesday*

Gary Colby

When our other preacher left our church
For a bigger church and better pay,
We had to find another preacher
To fill in right away

We had a few part time preachers
And *Gary Colby* was amongst those few,
Gary said that he would never again be a fulltime preacher
So we went on getting along with the best of what we could do

And as we continued surviving with part time help
They called up *Gary Colby* to help us out again,
And he said that he would for one condition and one condition only
When will my full time begin?

Praise the *Lord* and hallelujah
We got the one we were praying for,
Gary has a very good sense of humor
And a love within his heart for others and so very, very much more

I know that everyone praised the *Lord* that day
So happy that Gary changed his mind,
And he has promised to never let us down
There is no greater preacher that we could ever find

Since he came to us
Our church has doubled in number,
So many are using their *God*-given gifts and talents
To the praise of the one who never slumbers

Preaching and teaching and reaching out
And music galore,
Oh *Salem* of *Wilmot, God* has filled you to the full
We could not have asked for anything more

P.T.L. #1707 10-13-2019 *Sunday*

About the Author

Thomas Kruger has been writing for forty-two years with thirteen books being published as of now, most of these are Christian poems.